Playing with Words: A Poetry Writing Workshop

Karen Hamilton Silvestri

Karenzo Media

Playing with Words: A Poetry Writing Workshop

Karenzo Media

North Carolina, USA

Queensland, Australia

www.karenzomedia.com

Layout: Karen Hamilton Silvestri

ISBN 978-0-9899318-3-0

THE POET'S IDEA NOTEBOOK

Poet's record emotion more than anything else. What cannot be expressed by the telling, the poet seeks to tell by using everday objects, places, and people to get across an emotion. It is highly recommended that you keep a notebook of some sort that you can jot down ideas as they come to you.

Think of your notebook as your portable filing cabinet. **Good writers throw NOTHING away**. You may never use what you put in your Idea Notebook, but the act of keeping ideas will help to generate more ideas! Get in the habit of carrying it with you always, as you never know when you'll want to jot something down before it's forgotten.

This workbook contains blank ruled pages where you can try out the exercises or make notes as you read the exercises. Don't be afraid to write in your workbook! Many of these exercises come straight from my own poet's notebooks that I have kept over the years!

Suggested ideas for your notebook

People Watching - observations about the people around you

Eavesdropping - re-creations of conversations you hear

Descriptions - descriptions of the world around you

New words you encounter

Reflections - thoughts and feelings regarding your day

Poetry - other peoples or your own

Dreams (Yours or your buddy's! No one is safe from an artist!)

Found stuff - lines from novels or movies

First Lines and titles - first lines or titles for poems, stories, or other pieces

Quotes - cool quotes you hear or read

Part One: For the Younger Crowd

SENSORY IMAGERY – THE 5 SENSES

Sight * Sound * Smell * Touch * Taste

You try! Look at the following image. Transport yourself to the location in the image. Now close your eyes and ask yourself, "What do I see? What do I hear? What do I taste? What can I touch and what does it feel like? What do I smell?"

And finally, ask yourself, "How do all of these senses make me *feel*?"

Now fill out the chart below.

I see…	
I hear…	
I can touch…	
I smell…	
I taste…	
I feel…	

Finally, remove all of the word prompts, so that you end up with a poem similar to this one:

With word prompts	**After removing the word prompts**
I see a solitary biker riding in the surf	solitary biker riding in the surf
I hear the waves breaking on the shore	waves breaking on the shore
I can touch the wet sand under my feet	wet sand under my feet
I smell the fish enjoying the sea	fish enjoying the sea
I taste the salt in the ocean air	salt in the ocean air
I feel calm and happy	calm and happy

USING DESCRIPTORS

Descriptors (appositives) are phrases that add more information, more description to a simple sentence or phrase. Poetry is all about using description to describe an emotion, and using descriptors will help you do just that!

She wanted to go to the ocean, that beautiful deep blue water with seagulls flying low catching jumping fish.

You try! Read the model, and then complete the phrases with your own appositives.

MODEL: I wanted to go to that place--that place with people everywhere and loud music playing.

I wanted to go to that place, _____

MODEL: I was thinking of my favorite pet, that cute little Chihuahua with the big brown eyes that seemed to laugh when she was happy.

I was thinking of my favorite pet, _____

MODEL: Everything I care about---my baby sister with the funny laugh, my room that I painted blue, the cat snoring,--might be lost tomorrow.

All that I care about _____ --might be lost tomorrow

Group Activity: Create one model sentence like the ones you see above. Don't add the descriptor; just draw a blank where the descriptor belongs. Pass your sentence to the person next to you and have them come up with a descriptor for your sentence. That person then passes the paper to the next person and so on. Share with the class all the different sentences you end up with..

METAPHORS AND SIMILES

Simile: Comparing two unlike things using the words "like" or "as"

Metaphor: Comparing two unlike things not using "like" or "as"

Anger is _____ Anger is like a big red balloon about to burst.
(simile) Anger is a big red balloon about to burst. (metaphor)

My family is _____ My family is like a spicy casserole. (simile) My family is
a spicy casserole. (metaphor)

You try! You will come up with 5-10 similes and then 5-10 metaphors as fast

as you can. Compare each idea or emotion to a concrete object. A concrete object is
something you can touch (a pot, a table, an ocean, etc. Fill in the blanks as fast as you
can. If you can't think of anything, skip it and go on the next one. Compare each
emotion or idea to a concrete, specific **object**. The more detailed you can get, the
better!

1. Anger is _____

2. Love is _____

3. Fear is _____

4. Homework is _____

5. Summer is_____

6. My mother is _____

7. Life is_____

8. I am_____

9. Joy is _____

10. Shame is _____

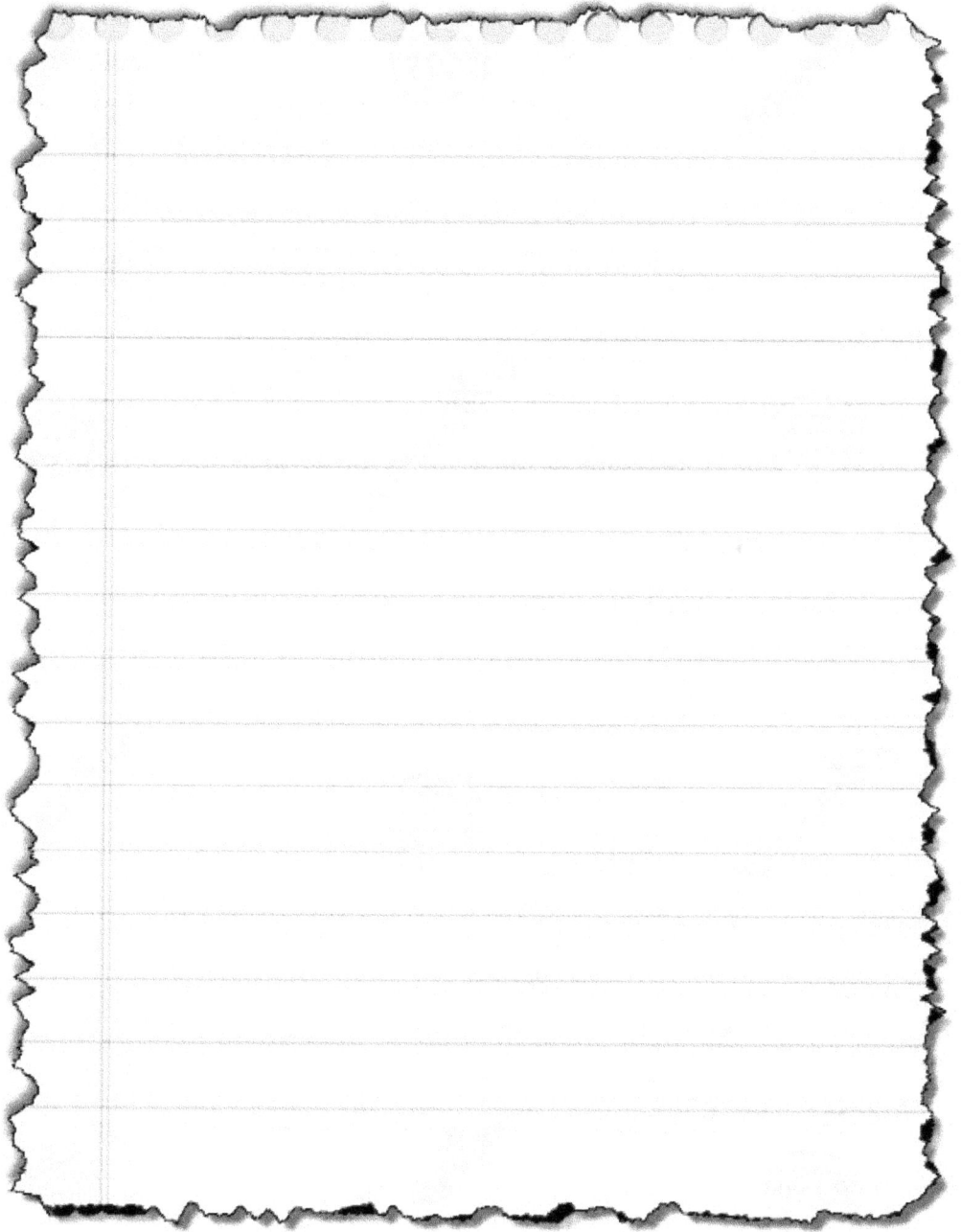

PERSONIFICATION

Personification is a language device in English where the writer gives a human quality to something that is not human.

Example:

"The flowers danced in the garden." The verb 'danced' is something that humans do, but here it is attributed to nonhuman flowers.

Now you try!

Directions: You are given below a list of objects and a list of action verbs. Working alone or with a group, combine objects with verbs and make sentences from what you choose. Share with the class.

Wind	Watched
Sun	Sang
Forest	Whispered
Ocean	Making
Books	Beat
Trees	Walked
Shoes	Called
Words	Died
Balloons	Withered
Storms	Gazed
Flowers	Wailed
Moon	Cried
Flowers	Laughed

You try! Play with the personification sentences you and your classmates created and write a poem based on one or two of the images. You may add as many words and lines to the poem as you wish, but you must use at least one of the personification sentences you created!

RHYMING

Scanning – When we match up the words that rhyme at the end of each line, we call this scanning.

I met a traveller from an antique land	a
Who said: "Two vast and trunkless legs of stone	b
Stand in the desert. Near them on the sand,	a
Half sunk, a shattered visage lies, whose frown	b
And wrinkled lip and sneer of cold command	a
Tell that its sculptor well those passions read	c
Which yet survive, stamped on these lifeless things,	d
The hand that mocked them and the heart that fed.	c

The rhyme scheme of this stanza is written this way: ababa cdc

See if you can scan the next stanza.

And on the pedestal these words appear:
`My name is Ozymandias, King of Kings:
Look on my works, ye mighty, and despair!'
Nothing beside remains. Round the decay
Of that colossal wreck, boundless and bare,
The lone and level sands stretch far away".

You try ! Write a rhyming couplet first and then write a poem.

Example: The sun shone bright in the sky
        It was a day when nothing would die.

Write at least six lines that describe your favorite place and what it means to you. Use end rhymes like those in the poem above. When you are finished writing, scan your poem and share it with the class

Repetition – Repeating Phrases

Another way to produce a musical rhythm in your poem is to repeat phrases.

You try! Using the phrase given below, write as many lines as you can that fill in the blank.

I never want to forget

_____.

I never want to forget

_____.

I never want to forget

_____.

I never want to forget

_____.

I never want to forget

_____.

I never want to forget

_____.

I never want to forget

_____.

I never want to forget

_____.

I never want to forget

_____

CINQUAIN

A cinquain is a five-line poem that describes a person, place, or thing.

> **beach**
> **hot, sandy**
> **sunning, tanning, swimming**
> **the best place to be**
> **vacation**

To write a cinquain poem choose the following for each line:
Line 1: a one-word title, a noun
Line 2: two adjectives
Line 3: three words ending in -ing
Line 4: a phrase
Line 5: a synonym for your title, another noun

You try!

1_____

a one word title, a noun that tells what your poem is about

2_____, _____

two adjectives that describe what you're writing about

3_____, _____, _____

three words ending in -ing that describe what your poem is about

4_____

a phrase that tells more about what you're writing about

5_____

a synonym for your title, another noun that tells what your poem is about

Acrostic Poem

1. Select a topic for your poem.

2. Write the topic word vertically on your paper. (Be sure to capitalize each letter of the word.)

3. Start each line of the poem with the capital letters you wrote.

4. Each line of the poem should consist of a word or phrase related to the topic. See the example below using the word *poem*.

Play with words
Open your mind
Everything is possible
My, what a great poem I wrote!

You try!

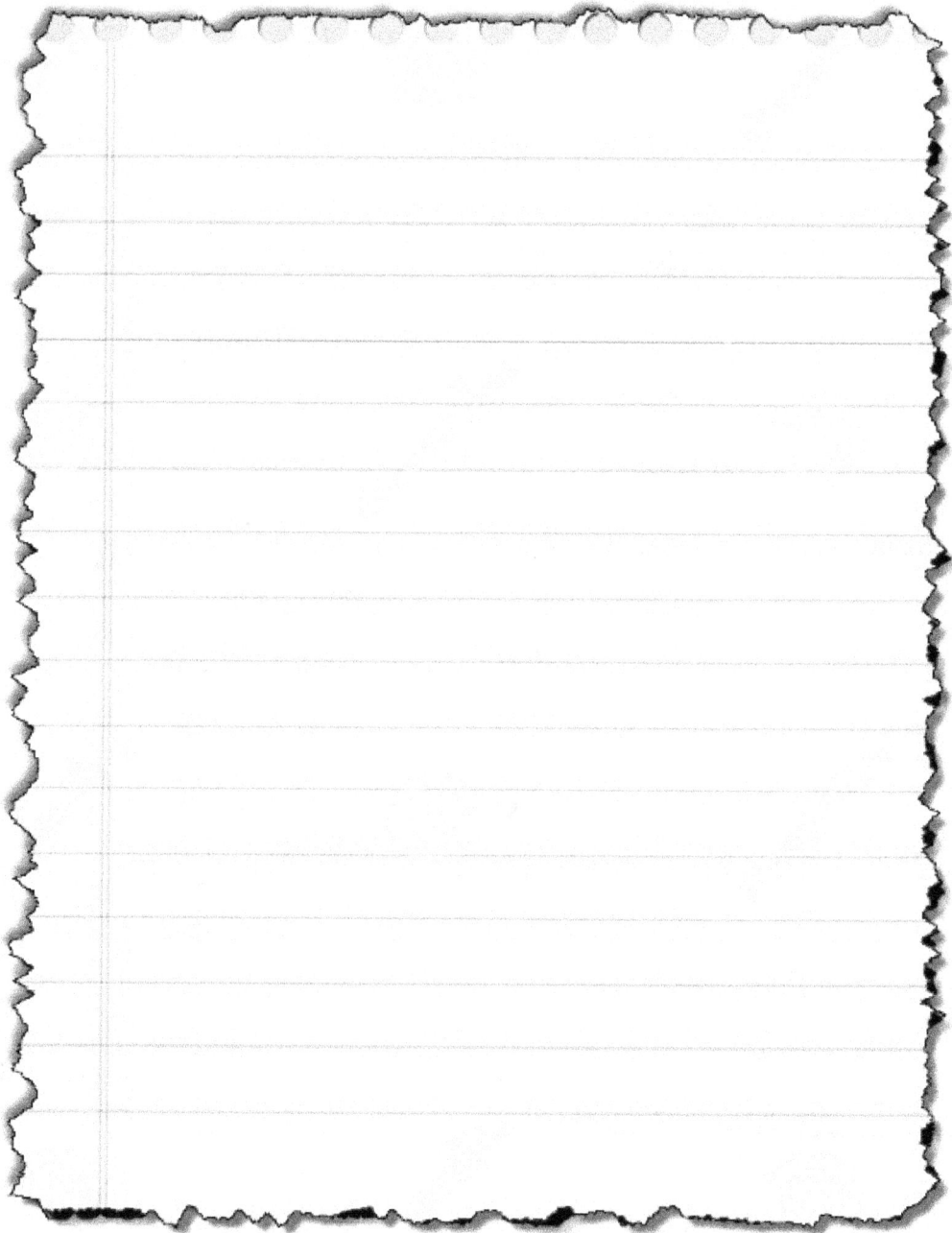

Haiku

- The origins of the Haiku come from Japan in the early 19th century and is a verse poem written with three lines.
- Haiku poems don't rhyme but rather use imagery to describe the topic.
- Haiku poetry has a composition of 17 syllables. The first line is five syllables, the second line is seven syllables, the third line and final line has five syllables. 5-7-5
- These poems are usually about ordinary things in nature.

To start creating a haiku, begin by choosing a subject. You can DESCRIBE your subject, tell how the subject makes you FEEL, or make an OBSERVATION about your subject. Think about your theme and some key words about your topic. Organize your thoughts roughly onto three lines:

It may take some playing around with the words to get the syllables to fit in the right order. Although the pattern is usually 5- 7- 5, it does not necessarily have to follow this pattern.

Practice: Scan the following haiku like the one in the box.

I saw through the door

Out into my big back yard

Birds were in the sky

You try! Write a Haiku that describes your bedroom or your back yard.

Sample Haiku

The red blossom bends
And drips its dew to the ground
Like a tear it falls

======================

Line 1: 5 syllables
The/ red/ blos/som/ bends

Line 2: 7 syllables
And/ drips/ its/ dew/ to/ the/ ground.

Line 3: 5 syllables
Like/ a/ tear/ it/ falls

CHILDHOOD PLACES

Memories of places we've been as children are great sources of material for a poem.

Carlin Park

I remember Carlin Park in the summer.
Long hot sandy beaches and sea grapes
waving in the ocean breeze.
Seagulls chasing crabs in the sand
and sunburned children chasing seagulls

We played softball in the park while
other kids hung out by the swings
flirting and eating burnt hot dogs.
As darkness fell, we gathered together
for a long game of King tag, hide and seek

Carlin Park was our summer home--
A place to laugh and love and live.

You try! Use sensory imagery to describe a place from your childhood. Make your poem at least two stanzas of five lines each.

End your poem with a couplet (two lines).

You are free to use rhyme or repetition to give your poem 'music'.

I am the One Who Poem

Sample

I am the one who answered the phone that night
I am the one who will always remember the look on my mother's face
I am the one who my father clung to
I am the one who notified relatives
I am the one who answered the door when the neighbors came
I am the one who ordered the flowers
I am the one who read the scripture at the mass
 I am the one who found telltale signs in his room
I am the one who should have tried harder to stop him
I am the one whose brother died of an overdose

You try! Complete each statement with a fact about yourself. Each line should lead up to the last line (the punchline) or main idea. I suggest you think of the last line first. Try to write at least 10 lines.

I am the one who

_____

_____.

I am the one who

_____

_____.

Some suggestions:

When someone got married
When someone was born
When someone or a pet died
When you went to a new school
When you got in a fight with someone
When you learned a life lesson

GENERATED POEMS

Generated Poems are all the rage these days. If you were to Google "generated poems" you would find hundreds of sites where you can write your own poem using prompts from the computer.

You try! Choose one of each. Try to NOT look at the second part of this exercise yet!

A color	
A place	
A person	
A verb (present tense)	
An adjective	
Another adjective	
Another adjective	
A noun	
An adjective ending in -ing	
Another noun	
An animal (singular)	
Another color	

Part Two Generated Poem Exercise

Now put each of the words you chose into the following blanks:

_____ skies over _____ again
    (1st color)   (place)

_____ arrives, _____ about
    (person)   (present tense verb)

Looking _____ and _____
         (1st adjective)   (2nd adjective)

The only _____ part – that _____
        (3rd adjective)   (1st noun)

_____ near _____
    (-ing verb)   (2nd noun)

Where _____ awaits
       (animal)

Now _____ _____
    (2nd color)   (repeat 1st noun)
Into _____ beginnings
    (repeat 1st color)

Then _____ once more
    (repeat 2nd color)

Blue Tree Staring
red skies over home again
mother arrives, blinks about
looking pretty and cold
the only silent part - that tree
staring near silence
where cat awaits

now blue trees fade
into red beginnings

FOUND POETRY

Where do you find

the Dream that CHANGES YOU

When will you feed your soul

Found poetry is just that - found. It is an exercise in letting your subconcious take over to find a poem you didn't even know was in you. The results can be quite stunning! This exercise can be combined with art work, which just makes it even more interesting.

You try!

Take an old book or a magazine and rip out a page or two. Quickly circle some of the words on the page that jump out at you or you find interesting.

Option #1: Cut out the words and arrange them on the page to form a poem.

Option #2: Use a marker or paint to block out all the words except the ones that you circled.

Don't worry about rhyming or making sense – just find words you like and put them together on a page!

Places for Kids to publish

Always look up the submission requirements of each magazine before submitting.

Amazing Kids eZine

Writers ages 5-17 may submit poetry, stories, book reviews, movie reviews, music reviews, essays, articles, etc. Both fiction and non-fiction are welcome.

The Blue Pencil Online

Edited and produced by the students in the Writing & Publishing Program at Walnut Hill, The Blue Pencil Online publishes verse, short fiction, and playwriting in English by young writers (ages 12-18) around the world.

Claremont Review

A magazine showcasing inspiring young adult writers ages 13-19.

Cicada Magazine

For youth readers 14-21. All ages submissions.

Creative Kids

Creative Kids magazine is the nation's largest magazine by and for kids with games, stories, and opinions all by and for kids ages 8–14.

Stone Soup

Fiction, poetry, illustrated stories, illustrations by youth under 13.

The Writer's Slate

The Writers' Slate online publishes original poetry and prose from students enrolled in kindergarten through twelfth grade.

Part Two: Advanced Poetry Writing for Teens & Above

By concentrating on the sounds, on the quality of the verbal music, and the strangeness of the juxtapositions rather than on the "meaning," one often comes closer to the secret language of the unconscious." – Steven Kowit

In the Palm of Your Hand: the Poet's Portable Workshop. Maine: Tilbury House, 1995.

Nuts and Bolts

Line and Stanza Breaks:

Drop one line to indicate a comma

Drop a stanza to indicate period

Hear where your line breaks

When writing poetry as narrative, a line break should create a pause in your story. Think of this pause as a transition from variations of emotions. You may move from peace to uncertainty to anger to peace again.

Repetition and Rhyme

Repetition is the 20th century version of rhyme

Tense

Present tense is always more effective in poetry

Cutting words

Get rid of every 'to be' verb and 'have/have not' type verbs

Get rid of prepositions, articles, etc. They don't do any work for your poem!

THE SHAKESPEAREAN SONNET

The Shakespearean sonnet has undergone many transformations over the years. The original form is three quatrains (4 lines) followed by a couplet. The rhyme scheme is abab, cdcd, efef, gg. The couplet is important as it sums up the poem and brings it to a conclusion. It might refute the quatrains or it might offer an epiphany. Whichever you end the sonnet, make sure the couplet at the end packs a punch!

My mistress' eyes are nothing like the sun (Sonnet 130)

by William Shakespeare

My mistress' eyes are nothing like the sun;
Coral is far more red than her lips' red;
If snow be white, why then her breasts are dun;
If hairs be wires, black wires grow on her head.

I have seen roses damasked, red and white,
But no such roses see I in her cheeks;
And in some perfumes is there more delight
Than in the breath that from my mistress reeks.

I love to hear her speak, yet well I know
That music hath a far more pleasing sound;
I grant I never saw a goddess go;
My mistress when she walks treads on the ground.

And yet, by heaven, I think my love as rare
As any she belied with false compare.

THE PERTRARCHAN (OR ITALIAN) SONNET

Petrarchan (or Italian) sonnet

The Petrarchan Sonnet is commonly used to make an observation, present an argument, or ask (and answer) a question. It consists of two stanzas followed by a sestet. The first stanz is an octave (8 lines). The octave leads into some sort of answer to the question or observation posed in the octave and should become more intense or most important in the last line (the volta). The second stanza of 6 lines (sestet) answers the first stanza in some way.

The rhyme scheme is abba, abba, cdecde or cdcdcd

"Scorn Not the Sonnet"

by Wordsworth

Scorn not the Sonnet; Critic, you have frowned,
Mindless of its just honours; with this key
Shakespeare unlocked his heart; the melody
Of this small lute gave ease to Petrarch's wound;
A thousand times this pipe did Tasso sound;
With it Camoens soothed an exile's grief;
The Sonnet glittered a gay myrtle leaf
Amid the cypress with which Dante crowned

His visionary brow: a glow-worm lamp,
It cheered mild Spenser, called from Faery-land
To struggle through dark ways; and when a damp
Fell round the path of Milton, in his hand
The Thing became a trumpet; whence he blew
Soul-animating strains--alas, too few!

My attempt at a Petrarchan Sonnet:

This was hard choice for me. There are several things that I wanted to describe. I wrote about a hope chest my grandfather gave to me. My original poem was written from a

The Hope Chest

Papa gave it to her on her sixteenth birthday
Dark varnished wood with engraved eagle face
She filled it with dishes and quilts made of lace
Treasures for a future she dreamed of someday.
Years went by and with time came decay
Beaten brass screws fallen and lost someplace
The eagle lid no longer connected to its base
Its treasures spilling over and tumbling away.

Here's a pewter salad spoon with no mate
And crochet blankets crocheted by a child,
A musical teapot that refuses to play
Memories with no more promises to create
Empty now and passively waiting to be filled
Dreams, memories and come what may.

freewrite describing how I got the chest and what I filled it with over the years, and then how it lost its items and got beat up because I moved so many times. The chest became in the writing a metaphor for life itself - how you get banged up as you age but you keep going and come out stronger.

You try!

Write either a Shakespearean sonnet or a Petrarchan sonnet using the theme of Family Heirlooms or Traditions. Don't stress too much about it; just try to keep the form and rhyme scheme going

DIGITS

Adapted from poet Steve Kowit, *In the Palm of Your Hand: The Poet's Portable Workshop*

There are many variations with this poem. Commonly called a cut-up or random poem, you can customize the rules any way that you want.

You try! Write out your birthdate (or the birthday of someone you love) in numbers. For example, 6/20/62

Using any dictionary, look up the first word and the last word on each page number listed in your birthday.

You can make up your own rules regarding the numbers! Create your own digits rules.

EXAMPLE

For this example, I choose to use a Spanish/English dictionary, but I only chose the English words.

6/20/62 = pages 6, 20, 62

Page 6 =pinch, fluster

Page 20 = authentic, yesterday

Page 62 = detach, description

Add the first two numbers. 6 + 20 = 26

Page 26 = bombard, brief

Add the last two numbers. 20 + 62 = 82

Page 82 = miscount, hiding

Add the first and last numbers. 6 + 62 = 68

Page 68 = doomsday, differ

Finally, multiply the first two numbers.

6 * 20 = 120

Page 120 = England, immunize

Sample poem:

England was briefly bombarded
with flusters of detached details
that differed greatly.
Yesterday they miscounted the
Doomsday disaster
Too many were in hiding
from authentic reality
Their descriptions pinched and pulled from immunized boxes

Remember, we are playing! You are free to add words and change tenses as you work on your poem.

Write a poem using the words on your list. How long should the poem be? You decide!

Optional Group work:

Each group should create a system of rules like those above. They can choose to a dictionary, a thesaurus, or any other book as a resource for the words. Exchange systems with other groups and see what everyone creates!

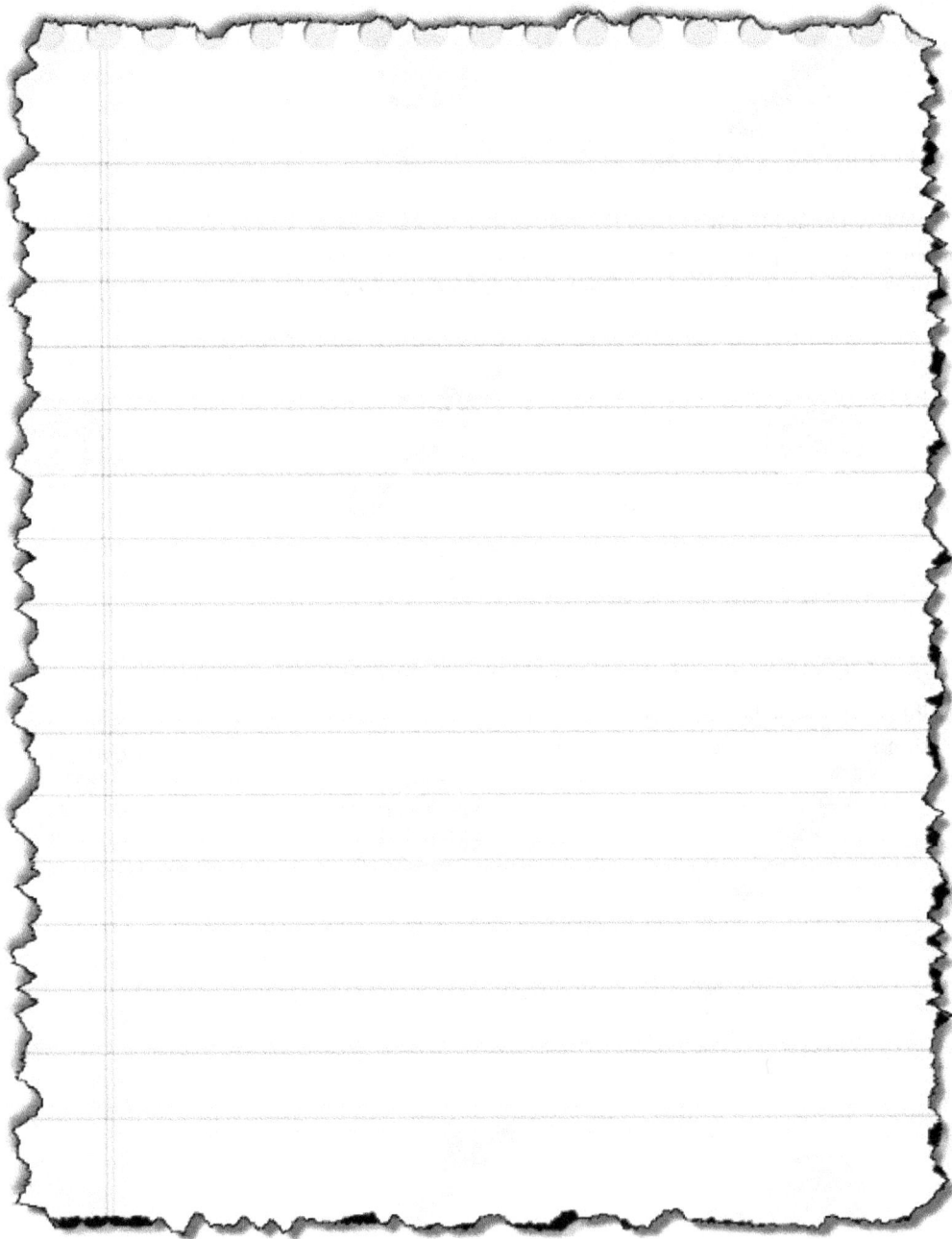

THE VILLANELLE

The highly structured villanelle is a nineteen-line poem with two repeating rhymes and two refrains. The form is made up of five tercets followed by a quatrain. The first and third lines of the opening tercet are repeated alternately in the last lines of the succeeding stanzas; then in the final stanza, the refrain serves as the poem's two concluding lines. Using capitals for the refrains and lowercase letters for the rhymes, the form could be expressed as: A1 b A2 / a b A1 / a b A2 / a b A1 / a b A2 / a b A1 A2.

Do not go gentle into that good night

by Dylan Thomas

Do not go gentle into that good night,
Old age should burn and rave at close of day;
Rage, rage against the dying of the light.

Though wise men at their end know dark is right,
Because their words had forked no lightning they
Do not go gentle into that good night.

Good men, the last wave by, crying how bright
Their frail deeds might have danced in a green bay,
Rage, rage against the dying of the light.

Wild men who caught and sang the sun in flight,
And learn, too late, they grieved it on its way,
Do not go gentle into that good night.

Grave men, near death, who see with blinding sight
Blind eyes could blaze like meteors and be gay,
Rage, rage against the dying of the light.

And you, my father, there on the sad height,
Curse, bless, me now with your fierce tears, I pray.
Do not go gentle into that good night.
Rage, rage against the dying of the light.
One Art

by Elizabeth Bishop

The art of losing isn't hard to master;
so many things seem filled with the intent
to be lost that their loss is no disaster.

Lose something every day. Accept the fluster
of lost door keys, the hour badly spent.
The art of losing isn't hard to master.

Then practice losing farther, losing faster:
places, and names, and where it was you meant
to travel. None of these will bring disaster.

I lost my mother's watch. And look! my last, or
next-to-last, of three loved houses went.
The art of losing isn't hard to master.

I lost two cities, lovely ones. And, vaster,
some realms I owned, two rivers, a continent.
I miss them, but it wasn't a disaster.

—Even losing you (the joking voice, a gesture
I love) I shan't have lied. It's evident
the art of losing's not too hard to master
though it may look like (Write it!) like disaster.

You try!

40

WORD SEARCH

Adapted from poet Steve Kowit, *In the Palm of Your Hand: The Poet's Portable Workshop*

The poet needs to be as surprised as the reader by the end of the poem. Let the poem surprise you." *-Ezra Pound, The ABC's of Reading*

This poem uses your subconscious to randomly find words that appeal to you for seemingly no reason. You will let your subconscious do most of the work as you prepare for this poem, so clear your head and prepare to let your inner you take over!

You try! **Materials Needed**: old newspapers and magazines, markers

Using two very different magazines and/or newspapers, you are going on a word search. I say *word*, but actually mean that you can also search for *phrases*. With your marker, circle words or phrases that jump out at you, words that make you pause, phrases that strike you for no reason at all.

Don't think about this! Just circle every time you feel yourself pause over a word or phrase. Don't spend too much time on one page. Circle a few things then go to the next page. Let yourself fall into a rhythm of *seeing* words but not really reading them or giving them any thought.

Do this with at least four pages from each magazine you chose. Now, go back and find the words you circled. Write them out on a piece of paper.

Once you have gathered all of your words and phrases, you are ready to begin writing your poem. You are free to add words and change tenses. You may end up not using all of the words that you circled, but be sure to give them a chance to fit in. Sometimes a word we think won't possibly work ends up tying the whole poem together!

Remember that your poem doesn't have to make complete sense, but the phrases that you create do need to have something to do with one another. We are searching for the rhythm, the music in the sounds!

Let your found words sing. You will be surprised how taking random words and phrases often leads to a quite coherent piece.

A Sample Word Search Poem

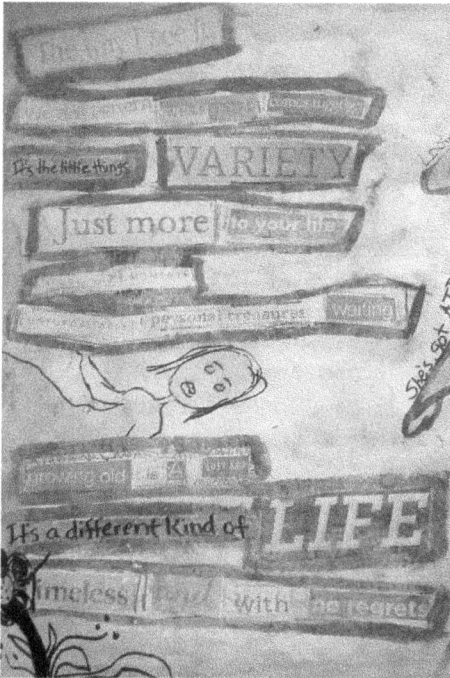

My Poem

The way I see it,

We're a pattern where life comes together

It's the little things - variety

Just more to your life

A mix of patterned moments

Unforgettable personal treasures waiting

Growing old is a lost art

It's a different kind of life

Timeless and with no regrets

THE CUT - UP POEM

This poem is similar to Word Search and Found Poetry, but I personally like this one the best! It requires you to tap into your subconcious and rely on your intuition rather than your concrete mind. It is a great way to loosen up when you are feeling stuck or have writer's block.

You try!

In this exercise, I want you to find your favorite book - your favorite story of all time. When I did this exercise, I had just finished reading "Wicked" by Gregory Macquire.

Grab a pen or pencil and some paper. Flip through the book and write on your paper (not in the book!) any phrases or sentences that strike you as interesting . once you have a list of 50 or so phrases, type them up into a document.

Now, look at the phrases and see if you can arrange them into a poem. Like the Word Search and Found Poetry poems, you will find that many of the phrases you chose can be combined to make whole new meanings!

Here is a sample of my poem from "Wicked":

Incomplete Wickedness

He called her Fabala
An imp spoiled the baby
Colored the child green,bless her soul
Little Elphaba has a social pattern to conform to

Glinda practices spells, a pretty peach rising
She watched the sun bleed ice
while Elphie watched the full moon fall
Roses on black, mirror images

The true story is like the mythical ocean
The green child becomes wicked and knows
The dead have souls and home
is the place you're never forgiven

Elphaba burns a page
and calls forth the lost
Peeping through poppies, dreaming of home
She mistakes them for others

Dorothy was a dark shape, locked in those shoes
The broom burned, and it's not to be believed
She hurled the water
It became a celebrated event

The moon in season played a Gilliknise ballad
While winter washed over Kiamo Ko
And whispered
Who needs forgiveness?

The body apologies, forgive me
The lion roared, motherless cub quaking,
He alone understands she didn't want
to be saved, mercy killing

Everything flickered, heels clicked together
They become others, their stories are over
There was never anything but straw
The scarecrow knows there is no happily ever after

NOTE: I did not finish this poem. It could be reworked to straighten out line length and stanza length, etc. But I think it has great potential, don't you?

SOLITAIRE

Adapted from poet Carol Muske, *The Practice of Poetry*

In this exercise you will let your mind create mental images of abstract words. Abstract words are words that mean something different to different people; such as, love, hate, war, soul, etc.

You try! Close your eyes and randomly choose a word from the list below. Just let your finger fall on one word. Look at your word, then close your eyes again and let images form in your head. Jot down the images on your paper.

Don't worry if the images that appear seem to have nothing to do with the word you chose. Write the image down anyway.

An example: I chose the word *love*. **Love:** heart, trees, beach, shells, sun, sky, blue, hands. These are the images that popped into my head as I thought of the word love. Spend a few minutes continuing this process until you have 20 words or so.

Using the images that you found, begin playing with forming lines from those words. Feel free to add words and change tenses as you need to. It is not necessary to use all of the images. Try to find a connection of these images to the word that you chose.

http://mrsjackiekelly.wordpress.com/list-of-abstract-nouns/

Love	Bravery	Beliefs
Hate	Loyalty	Dreams
Anger	Honesty	Justice
Peace	Integrity	Truth
Pride	Compassion	Faith
Sympathy	Charity	Liberty
Progress	Success	Knowledge
Education	Courage	Thought
Hospitality	Deceit	Information
Leisure	Skill	Culture
Trouble	Beauty	Trust
Friendships	Brilliance	Dedication

Alternate: write out the abstract words on index cards – one word per card. Shuffle your deck of cards and lay out the card on the top. Use that word to generate images.

CLICHÉ MASH UP

The cliché mash up is similar to the metaphor mashup. In this exercise, however, we will use phrases that are so familiar that we have most likely heard them more times than we can count.

Cliché – a word, phrase, or gesture that has been used over and over again to the point where it is very familiar

---

Novice poets (and writers) often overuse clichés, but used as a starting point – a jumping off place – the cliché can take us in interesting directions.

Here are some clichés you probably know:

Old as the hills	Everything but the kitchen sink	There but for the grace of god
Raining cats and dogs	Excuse me for living.	To tell the truth
Smart as a whip	Dying of boredom	A tower of strength
Kicked the bucket	Federal case	Bigger than life
Around the clock	Proud as a peacock	

You try! Once you have prepared a list of clichés (search for more on the Internet if you need to), try mixing and matching parts of the clichés to see what you come up with. Then use those new phrases to compose a poem of 5-10 lines.

Example Cliché Mash Up

He was as old as a whip
When he hit the truth
He had everything but the hills,
Where it was raining grace.
And the cat told him,
"Excuse me for dying."

MAKING HEADLINES

Headlines are everywhere. Did you know that people get paid just for writing headlines? In this exercise, we are going to look at some headlines in newspapers and magazines. Then we are going to PLAY with them! Of course.

You try! Gather some newspapers and magazines. Spread a few pages out on your desk. As always, we are not going to overthink this process; our task is to let our subconscious do the work for us.

With a marker, start circling headlines that catch your eye. Or you can tear out headlines that grab your attention for whatever reason. *I like the tearing out option because it allows you to then move the torn out headlines around on your desk.*

Play with the headlines you chose. Move them around, cut out words, add a word if needed….just PLAY!

Create new headlines from what you have chosen, headlines that express how you are feeling today, tell something that happened to you that you have been afraid or embarrassed to talk about, point out a solution to a social problem…you get the idea.

Alternate

Use the headlines that you found and create a news story about a common fairytale like The Three Little Pigs or Cinderella.

THE NARRATIVE POEM

Think of the narrative poem as a snapshot that tells a story. This is commonly called the lyric poem that has a lyrical sequence.

You can write several narrative poems that have a frame to tie them together. Your collection of poems can tell of a journey, be like a journal of a particular time period, or tell a story of a series of events.

The Language of Holding Up

This is the time they ask, *How are you holding up?*
Druggist, nurse, pastor, the kid who shovels snow,
and others you may hardly know or recognize,
but they know and they ask, and all you can say,

or are expected to say, is *OK. Doing the best I can.*
Meanwhile the checkout clerk at the supermarket
asks, *How are you today?* and you say *Fine. And You?*
These questions and their abbreviated replies beg

to be interpreted—as in, *What does Fine mean?*
Or *What is OK?* Besides a semi-literacy for *all right,*
however you spell it. All along, whatever the meaning,
faucets drip at slow intervals on a very cold night.

From *The Jane Poems*, by Ronald Moran

You try! Think of a time when something scary or upsetting happened to you. Tell the story in a narrative poem. You can use the sample poem as a model.

WRITING FROM EXHAUSTION

Adapted from Afterimages: The History of a Reflection by Jay Klokker

Sometimes the best poems come about after you have spent some time doing something physically exhausting. Robert Frost uses repetition in his poem below to write about an exhausting day in the fields.

After Apple Picking

by Robert Frost

My long two-pointed ladder's sticking through a tree
Toward heaven still.
And there's a barrel that I didn't fill
Beside it, and there may be two or three
Apples I didn't pick upon some bough.
But I am done with apple-picking now.
Essence of winter sleep is on the night,
The scent of apples; I am drowsing off.
I cannot shake the shimmer from my sight
I got from looking through a pane of glass
I skimmed this morning from the water-trough,
And held against the world of hoary grass.
It melted, and I let it fall and break.
But I was well
Upon my way to sleep before it fell,
And I could tell
What form my dreaming was about to take.
Magnified apples appear and reappear,
Stem end and blossom end,
And every fleck of russet showing clear.
My instep arch not only keeps the ache,
It keeps the pressure of a ladder-round.
And I keep hearing from the cellar-bin
That rumbling sound
Of load on load of apples coming in.
For I have had too much
Of apple-picking; I am overtired
Of the great harvest I myself desired.
There were ten thousand thousand fruit to touch,

Cherish in hand, lift down, and not let fall,
For all
That struck the earth,
No matter if not bruised, or spiked with stubble,
Went surely to the cider-apple heap
As of no worth.
One can see what will trouble
This sleep of mine, whatever sleep it is.
Were he not gone,
The woodchuck could say whether it's like his
Long sleep, as I describe its coming on,
Or just some human sleep.

You try!

Whether or not this really happened to Frost is beside the point. The point is to think of an event that was or could be physically demanding and draining and write about the feelings that the experience brings up.

Quickly make a list of experiences you have had when you felt totally drained. Choose one of these experiences and freewrite about it. Use as many adjectives, adverbs and vivid verbs as you can. Don't forget to use your senses!

Now step back from your freewrite and work on forming your thoughts into a poem. Look for words, thoughts, or ideas that repeat throughout your freewrite.

METAPHOR MASH UP

Adapted from *Everyday Creative Writing: Panning for Gold in the Kitchen Sink*

A **simile** compares two things using the words 'like' or 'as'

Her smile was as bright as the sun.

A **metaphor** compares two things without using the words 'like' or 'as'

Her smile was a sun shining brightly

Similes and Metaphors are the lifeblood of a poem. After all, poetry is about creating an image in words. It is about bringing inexpressible emotions to the world of language.

You try! In this exercise you will play with similes and metaphors. First, you will rearrange some similes, then you will turn those similes into metaphors (see the example above), and finally, you will create a poem from the created metaphors.

Here are some sample similes to get you started.

I'm sure you can think of more.

As radiant as…
As horrible as…
As quiet as…
Smiling like a …
Weeping like a …
Trembling like a …

Example of mixing simlies:

As crazy as a loon
As crazy as an old shoe
As tired as an old shoe
As tired as the moon
As big as the moon
As big as a loon

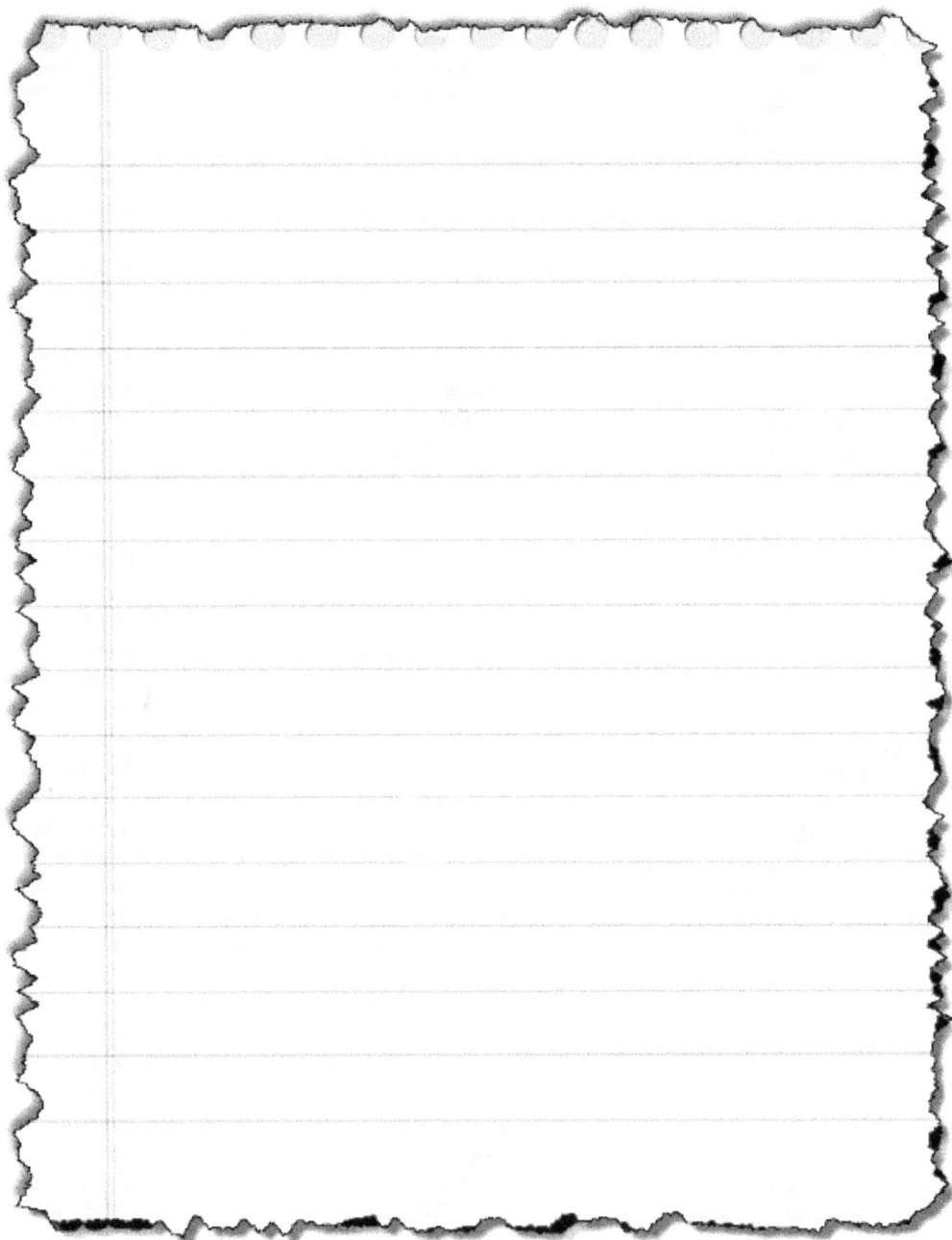

INKBLOTS

You're going to play with paint with this poetry writing exercise! Gather together some thick paper and acrylic paint and let's get started!

Once again we are going to not think too hard about this process. I want you to pick up whichever colors are calling to you and dribble some paint onto ONE SIDE of your paper. Write your name, a word, or just randomly drop blotches of paint.

Hint: you don't want the paint to be very thin but you also don't want a huge glob either.

Now, gently fold your paper over so that the two sides are touching. Carefully press down (not too hard!) so that the paint transfers to the other side. Unfold your paper and set it on your desk.

Here is the poetry part: Consider the inkblot you have created. Let your eyes see it out of the corner of your eye. What images do you see in your blot? Let these images play through your head and jot down words and phrases as you look. Take these images to words now and form a short poem.

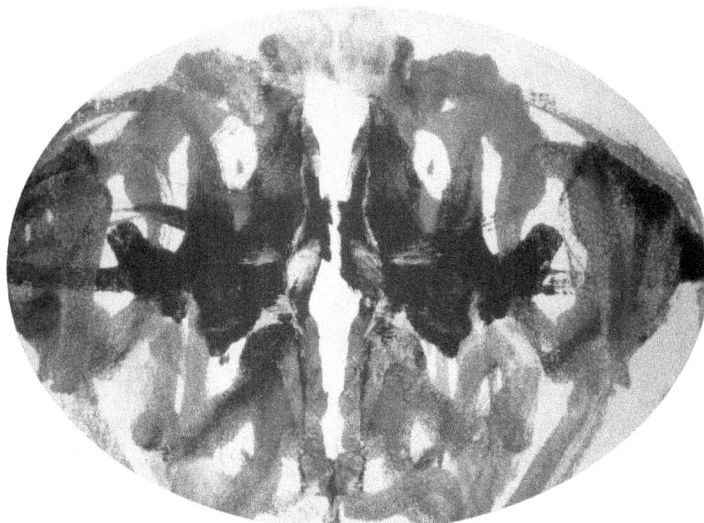

Here is my inkblot and the resulting poem.

It never was his idea
To be hunted
She chased him through fire
Through water through the sun
itself
It never was his idea
So they tumble eternally
The hunter and the hunted
Faceless horsemen always
looking
Forward not back
It never was his idea
To be the hunted

WONDERFUL WORLD OF NONSENSE

Take care of the sounds and the sense will take care of itself. – Lewis Carroll

Lewis Carroll was the master of nonsense language! Can you think of other poets and writers who played with language?

You try! In this exercise, you will join hands with the masters of language and create your own language. Think of three names of people in your life.

Lily, Jack, Micah

Now write out as many words as you can think of from the letters in those names.

Limick, Lijah, Jamily, Mijaly, Ackmicly

This is called **permutation,** and you may have encountered it in math class. Study each of your new words. Could they be used as nouns, verbs, adjectives, adverbs? Move them around and see if you can create a short poem like Carroll did in Jabberwocky. Notice that even though his words don't make sense, curiously they DO make sense because of the way they are used in the sentence.

Jabberwocky

by Lewis Carroll

'Twas brillig, and the slithy toves
  Did gyre and gimble in the wabe;
All mimsy were the borogoves,
  And the mome raths outgrabe.

"Beware the Jabberwock, my son
  The jaws that bite, the claws that catch!
Beware the Jubjub bird, and shun
  The frumious Bandersnatch!"

He took his vorpal sword in hand;
  Long time the manxome foe he sought—
So rested he by the Tumtum tree,
  And stood awhile in thought.

And, as in uffish thought he stood,
  The Jabberwock, with eyes of flame,
Came whiffling through the tulgey wood,
  And burbled as it came!

One, two! One, two! And through and through
  The vorpal blade went snicker-snack!
He left it dead, and with its head
  He went galumphing back.

"And hast thou slain the Jabberwock?
  Come to my arms, my beamish boy!
O frabjous day! Callooh! Callay!"
  He chortled in his joy.

'Twas brillig, and the slithy toves
  Did gyre and gimble in the wabe;
All mimsy were the borogoves,
  And the mome raths outgrabe.

SOUNDS LIKE

Onomatopoeia is a fun word all by itself! It is a device used to make words sound like what they mean.

Here are a few examples.

Whoosh

Buzz

Drip-drop-drip-drop

You try! Brainstorm some of your own words or brainstorm with others. Choose one or two of the words that you like the best and write a poem that uses those words.

Now, see if you can make your words LOOK like what they sound like!

Wh*ooshhhhhhhhhhhhhhh*

Buzzzzzzzzzzzzzzzzzzzz

Drip-

drop-

REPEATING PHRASES

I use sounds as it pleaes my own ear. And my ear likes lots of sound. Sound and repetition. I like "music" in poems. – Charles Wright

Add musical rhythm to your poem with repetition. There are many ways to add 'music' to your poems. One way is through rhyming and another way is by using repetition.

You try!

Use one of the phrases (or think of your own) below to write a repetition poem.

I will never forget…
I remember when…
I am the one who…
I need to…
Tomorrow is…
Don't ever tell…
Tell me this…

Try to let your writing hand simply move across the page as you repeat the phrase over and over in your head. Let your subconscious do the work.

Telling

Don't ever tell

that in her dreams there are

fantasies she can't speak of

Don't ever tell

that she wishes sometimes

to be alone and free

Don't ever tell

that sometimes she hears

a helicopter in her head

Don't ever tell

that sometimes she is so afraid

MAKING MUSIC

One form of repetition is called **alliteration**. Alliteration gives the poem a natural flow and rhythm that often sounds better to the ear than true rhyme.

Now old desire doth in his death-bed lie. – Romeo and Juliet

Alliteration is often used in myths and the Bible because it makes the passages easy to remember, which was important way back when writing had not been invented yet.

Tom the turkey traipsed to the tune of "Truly Trippin".

Notice all the T words used?

The repetition of consonant sounds is called ALLITERATION.

Lucy loves lurking under the low level lounge chair.

Notice all the L words?

You try! Rework one of your previous poems, paying close attention to the alliteration that is or is not present in your words. Try changing some of your words so they repeat vowels or consonants.

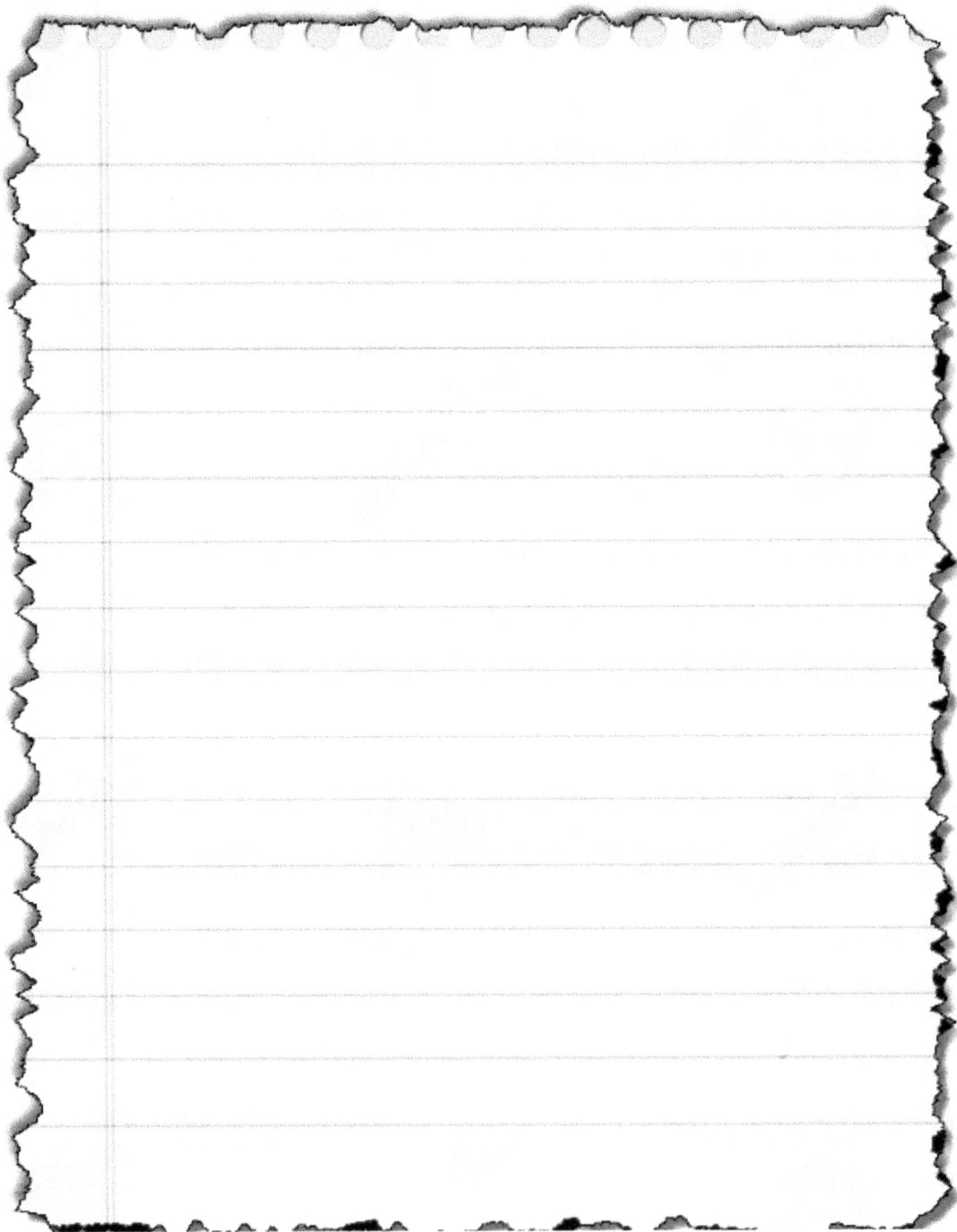

POEM GENERATORS

There are many places on the Internet that allow you to plug in some words and the computer will generate a poem for you.

Sometimes I will use these generators to kick start a poem. They are good sources of inspiration when you find yourself stuck.

Think Zone

http://thinkzone.wlonk.com/PoemGen/PoemGen.htm

Poetry Idea Engine

Get your poetry juices flowing with the Poetry Idea Engine. Created with GoCyberCamp, this activity will allow you to write haikus, free verse, limericks, and more!

http://teacher.scholastic.com/writewit/poetry/poetry_engine.htm#

Bibliography

Addonizio, Kim & Dorianne Laux. *The Poet's Companion: A Guide to the Pleasures of Writing Poetry*. New York: W. W. Norton and Company, 1997.

Bishop, Elizabeth. *One Art.*

Behn, Robin & Chase Twichell. *The Practice of Poetry*. New York: Haper Perennial, 1992.

Carroll, Lewis. *Jabberwocky*

Fox, John. *Finding What You Didn't Lose: Expressing Your Truth and Creativity Through Poem-Making*.New York: Penguin Putnam, Inc., 1995.

Frost, Robert. *After Apple Picking*

Hagberg, Janet O. *Wrestling with our Angels*. Massachusetts: Adams Publishing, 1995.

Kowit, Steve. *In the Palm of Your Hand: the Poet's Portable Workshop*. Maine: Tilbury House, 1995.

Moran, Ronald. *The Language of Holding Up*. The Jane Poems.

Shakespeare, William. *My mistress' eyes are nothing like the sun (Sonnet 130)*   .

Silvestri, Karen. *The Hope Chest, Telling, The Hunted, Carlin Park*

Smith, Michael C., & Suzane Greenberg. *Everyday Creative Writing: Panning for Gold in the Kitchen Sink*. Illinois: NTC Publishing Group, 1996.

Thomas, Dylan. *Do not go gentle into that good night.*

Wordsworth, William. *Scorn Not the Sonnet.*

Also try:

Fiction Writing Workshop for Teens: Review and Practice Worksheets for Middle and High School Students

Creative Writing Workshop for Middle & High School Students

Poetry Writing Workshop: A Workbook for Students

Short Story Writing Workshop: A Workbook for Students

Lifetales Workbook

Writing Your Memoirs Workshop: A Manual for Instructors

Lily's Adventures:2nd Grade Reader

The Caver King

Rock of Ages

Thief in the Night

The Time Card Series, Episode 1: Short Reads for Middle School

The Time Card Series, Episode 2 Declaration Time: Short Reads for Middle School

The Time Card Series, Episode 3 Rebooted: Short Reads for Middle School

The Time Card Series, Episode 4 Escape from Harvard: Short Reads for Middle School

The Time Card Series, Episode 5 Civil Rivalry: Short Reads for Middle School

Safe Counsel: A Complete Guide to Health Care and Home Remedies in the Late 19th Century

About the Author

Karen has published several non-fiction books and eBooks. Her specialty is memoirs, eBook writing/layout, and academic proofreading. In addition to teaching and freelance work, Karen also leads workshops in Creative Writing, Poetry and Journal Therapy, and Memoir Writing. She has studied genealogy and personal histories since 1987, lecturing and leading workshops on Memoir Writing and Journaling to the community since 1998. Karen holds a BA in English and has studied Literature, Business, and Education at the graduate level. She currently works at a community college in Lumberton, N.C. as an English instructor and Instructional Specialist. Email Karen at karenzomedia@gmail.com

Karenzo Media

www.karenzomedia.net

www.ingramcontent.com/pod-product-compliance
Lightning Source LLC
Chambersburg PA
CBHW080551030426
42337CB00024B/4836